A GIFT FOR.

....

FROM:

....

DISCOVER
PARADISE

DAVID
JEREMIAH

A GUIDEBOOK TO HEAVEN, YOUR TRUE HOME

COUNTRYMAN®

NASHVILLE, TENNESSEE

Project Editor: Pat Matuszak
Project Manager: Kathy Baker

Designed by Lookout Design, Inc., Stillwater, MN

ISBN 1 4041 0384 8

www.jcountryman.com | www.thomasnelson.com

Printed in the United States of America

TABLE OF CONTENTS

WELCOME TO PARADISE

Heaven Awaits You!

Welcome to Paradise! It's the place you've been dreaming of. Discover why it's the ultimate destination. This is IT! Nowhere on earth can compare. It's not just a getaway—once you have experienced the out-of-this-world facilities, you will find out why those who choose Paradise call it their heart's true home. And it's all just waiting for you.

Among the attractions of our perfect community are:

- Gleaming new homes with a comprehensive everlasting warranty
- Friends and family who are known for their love, joy, and celebration
- Management and staff who make sure your every need is fulfilled
- Glory-bright days and highest quality of life
- Life without night, sadness, sickness, or death
- The chance to bask in the undiluted Presence of the love of God forever.

You'll never need to carry a wallet or credit card; everything has already been paid for. All you have to do is make the choice to come. Your new dream home, best friends, cherished family, and dearest treasures will be waiting for you when you arrive. There's room here for everybody, so we hope you'll invite others to come along with you.

Paradise is Heaven. Make yourself at home! Reservations are unlimited, but time is running out, so RSVP today!

> The Bible is a super-natural book about a super-natural God who has a super-natural plan for His super-saints to live super-natural lives. We can learn more about Heaven from the Word of God than from someone who happened to come back from the dead (Luke 16:19-31). We need to know what the Bible says about our future home. *Discover Paradise* is not a theological treatise; instead, it's a biblically based "travel guide" that offers us a glimpse of Heaven and encourages us to make the most of the journey there.

ACTIVITIES IN HEAVEN:
What We'll Do

When you get to Heaven, you will enter a vibrant, growing community with activities that are exciting beyond all anticipation. This trip of a lifetime begins the moment you are escorted through the magnificent gates of the city. You'll stroll along crystal riverbanks, tour architectural wonders, and feast your eyes on spectacular gardens as you walk along avenues of gold.

You cannot begin to comprehend the beauty, purity, or grandeur of your heavenly destination. It's impossible to see it all in one day, so various tours are offered to get you acquainted with the delights of this amazing world

Tour Packages:

- *The City Gates Tour:* See the twelve Gates of Pearl sculpted by master craftsmen of the ages.
- *The City Walk Tour:* Navigate the city on foot viewing architecture, gardens, and sampling an endless variety of cuisine of all lands.
- *The Who's Who Tour:* Visit the homes of famous people and enjoy their hospitality, including Abraham, Moses, Esther, Ruth, Peter, John, and many more!

- *The Behind the Scenes Tour:* See how God did it! View Heavenly footage from the Creation of Heaven and Earth to the parting of the Red Sea, all the miracles of Jesus, and more.
- *The Throne Room Tour:* Enjoy as many hours as you wish in the presence of God Himself! Special Residents' Pass allows you return privileges so you can come back again and again, as many times as you like!

AND THERE IS MUCH MORE INCLUDED IN YOUR RESERVATION FOR PARADISE!

You'll be a guest at specially prepared banquets and attend sessions by the masters of art, music, worship, sports, and the wisdom of the ages. Take all the activities you like most about a vacation, wrap them all up in a residential community that lasts forever, and that's what you'll be experiencing in Paradise! You'll arrive rested and refreshed and ready to take on all the celestial City has to offer. Here are just a few of the many activities you can enjoy a la carte:

- *Dining Out:* Celestial cuisine is delicious beyond anything you've ever tasted. It is 100 percent fat free, so no matter how much you eat, it will never weigh you down.
- *Music:* From classical to karaoke, you'll find music everywhere in Paradise! Music Row goes on for hundreds of miles here and all styles are welcome. You'll sing like an angel and play any musical instrument like a virtuoso!
- *Social Events:* Catch up with friends and family you haven't seen in years! You'll have perfect understanding and harmony in God's light, and you'll spend eternity making new friends who are waiting to meet you.
- *Worship Opportunities:* The ultimate adventure of worshipping in the presence of the Creator and the saints of all the ages. It's not your granny's church meeting!

SAY GOODBYE TO BOREDOM FOREVER!

Unlike some recreational communities where people eventually become bored with the facilities, the endless variety of activities and new companions to enjoy them with in Heaven will both enrich your life and excite your curiosity.

In the hyperactive culture of the world, we often find a fear of boredom has taken hold in our hearts, so it's no wonder we put off making our reservation for Paradise. We may imagine it is like some of the more disappointing retreats or long-winded seminars we have attended on earth and think, "If I'm bored down here, what is it going to be like up there?"

Misinformation about Heaven permeates Mark Twain's books, especially his final work, *Extract from Captain Stormfield's Visit to Heaven.* After racing comets for thirty years Stormfield ends up at Heaven's entrance, but is puzzled when he receives none of the things he needs:

> *I lack my harp, and my wreath, and my halo, and my hymn-book, and my palm branch—I lack everything that a body naturally requires up here.*

Finally, properly outfitted, Stormfield observes:

When they gave me my kit and I put on my halo and took a look in the glass, I could have jumped over a house for joy, I was so happy. Now, I'm all right—show me a cloud.

After sixteen or seventeen hours of playing the only song he knows, Stormfield declares, "This AIN'T just as near my idea of bliss as I thought it was going to be. When challenged to learn a new song because "it's a long time to hang on to the one—eternity, you know," he replies:

Don't break my heart. I'm getting low-spirited enough already.

Stormfield didn't understand Heaven. The truth is that God, the giver of all good gifts, offers us so much more than a tedious existence among boring people. Heaven will be more exciting than a rollercoaster, more celebratory than Times Square on New Year's Eve, more heartwarming than a newborn baby, and all the fun will be open infinity / eternity. (There won't be any "24/7" limits because the light never fades.)

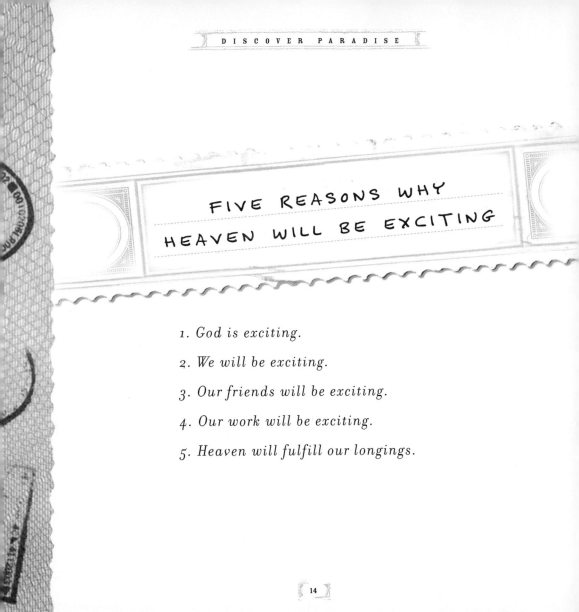

FIVE REASONS WHY HEAVEN WILL BE EXCITING

1. *God is exciting.*

2. *We will be exciting.*

3. *Our friends will be exciting.*

4. *Our work will be exciting.*

5. *Heaven will fulfill our longings.*

1. God is Exciting

You will show me the path of life:

In Your presence is fullness of joy;

At Your right hand are pleasures forevermore.

—Psalm 16:11

When we get to Heaven, we get near to God. At His right hand there are pleasures that go on forever. In His presence are fullness, completeness, and the absolute explosion of joy! Heaven is God's place, and God is not boring. People who talk about God might be boring, but God is the source of all good things—the taste of dessert, the adrenaline rush in our veins, the pleasure of sex, the expressive release of music and art, the laughter of children. God is the most exciting, adventuresome, creative person that we can imagine, multiplied a million times over. It goes off the radar screen. We can't even comprehend a little bit of the excitement that is resident in the Triune God with whom we will spend eternity forever and ever. That's where God is, and He's not boring!

2. WE WILL BE EXCITING

Behold, I (show) you a mystery: We shall not all sleep, but WE SHALL ALL BE CHANGED—*in a moment, in the twinkling of an eye, at the last trumpet. For the trumpet will sound, and the dead will be raised incorruptible, and* WE SHALL BE CHANGED.

—1 CORINTHIANS 15:51, 52 EMPHASIS ADDED

Twice in that verse, what does it say about us? We're going to be changed.

For our citizenship is in heaven, from which we also eagerly wait for the Savior, the Lord Jesus Christ, who will TRANSFORM OUR LOWLY BODY *that it may be conformed to His glorious body, according to the working by which He is able even to subdue all things to Himself.*

—PHILIPPIANS 3:20, 21 EMPHASIS ADDED

Heaven will not be boring because we will not be boring. Like the Lord, we will be exciting. When we get to Heaven, all of the reasons that we are boring now will be gone—reshaped into a perfect resurrection body. No matter how boring we might have been on this earth, there won't be one moment of boredom in our hearts when we get there.

3. OUR FRIENDS WILL BE EXCITING

Heaven will be exciting because our friends will be exciting.

> *But you have come to Mount Zion and to the city of the living God, the heavenly Jerusalem, to an innumerable company of angels, to the general assembly and church of the firstborn who are registered in heaven, to God the Judge of all, to the spirits of just men made perfect.*
>
> —HEBREWS 12:22, 23

As far as God is concerned, we are already seated with Christ in the heavenlies, and these are the people with whom we will spend all of eternity. It's pretty impressive to be on this guest list, is it not?

- We're going to spend eternity with all of the justified people made perfect; those are all of the Old Testament saints.
- We're going to spend eternity with the people who are of the firstborn; those are the church, the New Testament saints.
- We're going to spend eternity with the angels.
- We're going to spend eternity with God.

We're going to spend eternity with all of those who have been justified by the blood of Jesus Christ. Just as we will be changed when we are resurrected, so also will everyone else have been changed.

Jonathan Edwards, the Puritan writer, wrote this:

> *No inhabitants of that blessed world will ever be grieved with the thought that they are slighted by those that they love. Or that their love is not fully and fondly returned . . . There shall be no such things as flattery or insincerity in heaven, but there, perfect sincerity will reign through(out) all in all. Everyone will be just what he seems to be and will really have all the love (that) he seems to have. It will not be as it is in this earth where comparatively few things are what they seem to be and where professions are often made lightly and without meaning. But there, every expression of love shall come from the bottom of the heart, and all that is professed shall be really and truly felt.*

In Heaven it'll be total openness to one another with no fear of any reprisal, because we will be God's people made over, new, perfectly compatible with one another and able for the first time ever to enjoy that kind of intimate fellowship that we all long for in our hearts. Here we have a few moments like that, but in Heaven that's the way it's going to be forever.

One of the exciting things about Heaven will be the unlimited opportunity to fellowship with people of the various ages of history. When we're living together in Heaven, we can become fast friends with people we've only read about in books. People like David, Joseph, and Daniel. We'll walk along the streets of gold and say, "Oh, there's Joseph," and we'll share some angel food cake with Naomi. We can cultivate relationships with Paul the Apostle and John the Beloved. We will be able to personally thank C. S. Lewis, Charles Haddon Spurgeon, Andrew Murray, A. W. Tozer, and others who have inspired our faith.

Heaven's going to be such an incredible time of unlimited fellowship with people who have lived in all ages. We're going to live together in community and be able to fellowship with one another forever and ever and ever. And as great as all of this is, it pales into insignificance when it is compared to being in the presence of the Lord Jesus Christ who loved us and gave Himself for us.

4. OUR WORK WILL BE EXCITING

When we get to Heaven, we're going to be the servants of the living God. Servants work. They have an occupation. They have a responsibility. What is God going to say to us when we get to Heaven? He's not going to say to us, "Well done, good and faithful servant. Take the rest of eternity off." He's going to say, *"Well done, good and faithful servant . . . enter into . . ."* Into what? *". . . Enter into the joy of your Lord"* (Matthew 25:21). Why? *"You were faithful over a few things, I will make you ruler over many things."* God's got something for us to do.

Over and over, the book of Revelation repeats this thought of serving in Heaven.

> *Therefore they are before the throne of God, and serve Him day and night in His temple.*
> —REVELATION 7:15

> *And there shall be no more curse, but the throne of God and of the Lamb shall be in it, and His servants shall serve Him.*
> —REVELATION 22:3

. . . He sent and signified it by His angel to (the) servant John.

    —REVELATION 1:1

. . . Do not harm the earth, the sea or the trees, till we have sealed the servants of our God on their foreheads.

    —REVELATION 7:3

. . . That You should reward Your servants the prophets and the saints.

    —REVELATION 11:18

They sing the song of Moses, the servant of God . . .

    —REVELATION 15:3

Then a voice came from the throne, saying, "Praise our God, all you His servants and those who fear Him, both small and great!"

    —REVELATION 19:5

And the Lord God of the holy prophets sent His angel to show His servants the things which must shortly take place.

    —REVELATION 22:6

We Will Hear God Say, You're Hired!

In the millennial period (see page 26) we're going to rule and reign with Christ upon this reconfigured earth. But throughout eternity, we know that God has a great plan for every one of us to be wonderfully, happily, excitedly, and unboringly employed in serving Him. All of us will be serving in the fullest expression of the capacity God has given us and the giftedness He has put within us. However that works out in your life or in mine, we will discover it. Perhaps that's what Rudyard Kipling meant when he wrote these insightful lines of poetry:

> When earth's last picture is painted, and the tubes are twisted and dried,
> When the oldest colors have faded, and the youngest critic has died,
> We shall rest, and, faith, we shall need it—lie down for an aeon or two,
> Till the Master of All Good Workmen shall set us to work anew!

Let's think about this today: Everything we do, every ounce of energy we expend in our work in Heaven will last forever and ever. Forever and ever it will be a blessing and encouragement to all those who see it. What a legacy! Our work won't be boring; it will be exciting.

5. HEAVEN WILL FULFILL OUR LONGINGS

For we know that the whole creation groans and labors with birth
pangs together until now.

—ROMANS 8:22, 23

What does that mean? Paul was not writing here about unbelievers. He was talking about all of us as Christians, and he was saying that within us there is a hunger, a deep-down desire for something more. Even though we know Jesus and He has come to fulfill the major need in our life, there's still something missing because we haven't been fully redeemed. We have not yet experienced all that God has for us. And God has put within us this longing for something more.

Ecclesiastes tells us in the third chapter that God has put eternity in our hearts (v. 11). God has built us, as believers, with a space within us that can't be satisfied with anything except eternity, and no matter how many temporal things we try to put in that space, there's still a cavity from which springs our longing and yearning for something more.

God created all of us with this deep-seated hunger within us for Him and for Heaven, and it can never be fulfilled otherwise. No matter what we try, even as believers, as much as we serve and worship the Lord, our hearts still long for something more. And it's Heaven! Until we get to Heaven, we will never be whole.

When we get to Heaven, that inner ache is going to go away.

SATISFACTION GUARANTEED!

In Heaven, everything we do will bring us absolute, perfect satisfaction and reward. In Paradise, we'll never engage in anything that leaves us feeling even a tad bit empty. Everything we do will bring us absolute fulfillment and joy. We won't be bored in Heaven, because Heaven is everything we've been seeking.

Heaven is the answer to the deepest longings in our hearts. Only in Heaven will we finally feel the completeness that we were created to enjoy.

Because we hunger and thirst for excitement, adventure, and enjoyment, Heaven is the place to be.

MAKING SENSE OF THE MILLENNIUM

Almost everyone knows the lyrics to the Isaac Watts' famous hymn, "Joy to the World,"

Joy to the world! The Lord is come;
Let earth receive her King;
Let every heart prepare Him room,
And heaven and nature sing.

Joy to the earth! The Savior reigns;
Let men their songs employ;
While fields and floods, rocks, hills and plains,
Repeat the sounding joy.

No more let sins and sorrows grow,
Nor thorns infest the ground;
He comes to make His blessings flow
Far as the curse is found.

He rules the world with truth and grace
And makes the nations prove
The glories of His righteousness,
And wonders of His love.

but few people realize that it is really not a Christmas hymn. Look at the words. Did we receive Jesus as king at His first advent in Bethlehem? No. Has the curse of sin been removed? Do the nations prove His righteousness? Not yet. Only during the Millennium will the words to "Joy to the World" be fulfilled and sung with full meaning in our hearts as we reign with King Jesus on earth.

The Bible teaches that at the end of the present church age, the Rapture will occur when the dead in Christ are raised as He takes all Christians to Heaven. The Rapture ushers in a seven–year period known as the Tribulation, which culminates with the second advent—when Jesus returns to take up His reign on the earth. Satan will be bound during the period of the millennium (Revelation 20:2, 3). "Millennium" is a Latin term which is made up of two words: *mille*, which means "a thousand," and *annum* which means "years." *Mille annum*, "a thousand years." *During the millennial period God will . . .*

REWARD HIS PEOPLE

"For the Son of Man will come in the glory of His Father with His angels, and then He will reward each according to his works."

—MATTHEW 16:27

and events will . . .

RESPOND TO THE PROPHETS' PREDICTIONS

Of the increase of His government and peace There will be no end, Upon the throne of David and over His kingdom, To order it and establish it with judgment and justice From that time forward, even forever. The zeal of the Lord of hosts will perform this.

—ISAIAH 9:7

REVEAL THE ANSWER TO THE DISCIPLE'S PRAYER

"Your kingdom come. Your will be done. On earth as it is in heaven."

—MATTHEW 6:10

REEMPHASIZE MAN'S DEPRAVITY

Now when the thousand years have expired, Satan will be released from his prison and will go out to deceive the nations which are in the four corners of the earth, Gog and Magog, to gather them together to battle, whose number is as the sand of the sea.

—REVELATION 20:7, 8

What would it be like on this earth if all sin were removed for a thousand years? Profiles of the millennium: great peace, prosperity, purity, prolonged life, and personal joy. Be sure that you have made your RSVP so that you will experience these profiles of the millennium.

WORSHIPPING TOGETHER IN CHRIST

The book of Revelation makes it clear that massive gatherings of saints will celebrate in Heaven's worship experiences. Here's a sampling of of these.

Then I looked, and I heard the voice of many angels around the throne, the living creatures, and the elders; and the number of them was ten thousand times ten thousand, and thousands of thousands, saying with a loud voice:

"Worthy is the Lamb who was slain
To receive power and riches and wisdom,
And strength and honor and glory and blessing!"
    —REVELATION 5:11, 12

And I heard a voice from heaven, like the voice of many waters, and like the voice of loud thunder. And I heard the sound of harpists playing their harps. They sang as it were a new song before the throne . . .
    —REVELATION, 14:2, 3

And I heard, as it were, the voice of a great multitude, as the sound of
many waters and as the sound of mighty thunderings, saying,
"Alleluia! For the Lord God Omnipotent reigns!"

—REVELATION 19:6

If we enjoy choirs and orchestras here on this earth, imagine what it will be like when we hear the celestial choirs, accompanied by heavenly orchestras, lifting praise to Almighty God around the throne! And we will be a part of that in Heaven.

Worship is really "worth–ship"—ascribing to Jesus what is His by virture of His nature.

Corporate worship is necessary. We need the church! And we need each other. There is no such thing as individual Christianity. The word "saints" is always plural in the Bible.

CRESCENDO OF WORSHIP

Worship in Heaven just keeps getting bigger and better. It crescendos. In music, "crescendo" means to get louder and louder, to get bigger and bigger; to make more and more out of what started as small. A crescendo is to finish big! And the book of Revelation observes an obvious crescendo in praise and worship.

A TWO-FOLD DOXOLOGY:

". . . to Him be glory and dominion forever and ever. Amen."

—REVELATION 1:6

A THREE-FOLD DOXOLOGY:

"You are worthy, O Lord,
To receive glory and honor and power;
For You created all things,
And by Your will they exist and were created."

—REVELATION 4:11

A FOUR-FOLD DOXOLOGY:

And every creature which is in heaven and on the earth and under the
earth and such as are in the sea, and all that are in them, I heard saying:

"Blessing and honor and glory and power
Be to Him who sits on the throne,
And to the Lamb, forever and ever!"

—REVELATION 5:13

A SEVEN-FOLD DOXOLOGY:

"Blessing and glory and wisdom,
Thanksgiving and honor and power and might,
Be to our God forever and ever."

—REVELATION 7:12

In churches today, we also love to do that in our worship. We like to end big! We sometimes start small and keep changing keys as the music gets louder and bigger and mightier. That's biblical! That's going to happen in Heaven, and here on earth we're just rehearsing. Never in the history of Christianity has there been a greater emphasis on worship and praise than there is today. God's people are finding what it means to really worship God with all of their hearts and souls and minds, because one day that's how it's going to be in Heaven. Heaven will be a grand crescendo of worship throughout eternity.

START REHEARSING TODAY
FOR HEAVEN'S CHOIR

You and I are constantly bombarded with the reality of this world. Television, radio, and newspapers are incessantly getting us to focus on this world and on our present reality and all of its problems. Yet this reality is in contrast to the reality of Heaven. Christians often live as though the unseen eternal things are somehow less real than what we can see, but according to the Scripture, they are more real.

It is through worship that our spirits are lifted up into the heavenlies. It is through worship that we are made to see God as John saw Him. And it is through worship that our lives start to have a perspective that spares us from the rollercoaster rides that used to dominate us before we discovered what it is like to really worship Almighty God.

As we rehearse here on earth for the grand worship in Heaven, keep these things in mind:

1. *Worship is not about us—it's about Him!* Worship is to be offered up to the Lord from our heart, soul, and mind, knowing that the object of our worship is on the throne that we'll see when we look through the door in Heaven. Worship gets us in tune with God.

2. *Worship is not about here; it's about there.* One of the main purposes of worship is to get our minds off the things of this earth and onto the things in Heaven. And only as we're able to do that can we ever hope to function with integrity in our lives. When we see Heaven, earth starts to make more sense.

3. *Worship is not about now; it's about then.* Worship is the avenue that leads us from the emptiness of this world to the fullness of the next world. When we fail to worship, we confine ourselves to the despair of this life.

ATTRACTIONS IN HEAVEN:
What We'll See

PARADISE IS THE
PERFECT PLACE

All through the history of our race, this hope has emerged from time to time with the anticipation of an era when the earth would be at peace and at rest and we would experience a golden age.

This is exactly what the Lord Himself taught us to pray when He gave us the Lord's Prayer. When you pray the Lord's Prayer and you say, "Your Kingdom come. Your will be done on earth, as it is in Heaven" (Matthew 6:10), that is what you are praying for: that the conditions of Heaven will be found at last on this earth

But this is not going to happen during the current reign of mortality on this earth. Not ever. But this is the hope in every heart. This is the proper expectation of the people of God. This is what the writer of Hebrews had in mind when describing people who had suffered greatly and were managing to get through that suffering because they had a hope.

For those who say such things declare plainly that they seek a homeland . . . But now they desire a better, that is, a heavenly country.

—Hebrews 11:14, 16

Christians have a hope within them. And it is the hope for that eternal utopia that gets us through the tough times of suffering.

PARADISE IS LIKE EDEN . . . ONLY BETTER!

Consciously or unconsciously, we all yearn wistfully for the return of the Earth of Creation. In every person burns a desire for what our first parents enjoyed. We desire a perfect and a beautiful Earth. We want everything restored that was lost. We can't help ourselves. It's programmed into the software of our humanity. We want Paradise.

New Jerusalem is the crown of the new creation of God, but the New Jerusalem is not all of Heaven. New Jerusalem is the capital city of Heaven.

> *Then I John, saw the holy city, New Jerusalem, coming out of heaven from God, prepared as a bride adorned for her husband.*
> —REVELATION 21:2

God is preparing the holy city to be the final abode of His children, and when it's ready, it will come down out of Heaven. Revelation 3:12 calls this place, "the city of my God, the New Jerusalem, which comes down out of Heaven." It will be the most incredible city anyone has ever envisioned. It is this city that the Lord was talking about when He said to His disciples, "I go to prepare a place for you. And if I go and prepare a place for you, I will come again and receive you unto myself; that where I am, there you may be also" (John 14:2, 3).

What is the Lord Jesus doing now? He's working on our place. Some people call it a mansion; call it what you will, it is the part of that future that God is constructing for us right now.

Holiness is the chief characteristic of this city where we will one day live. Here on earth, Istanbul and Athens and San Diego are beautiful cities, but they are not holy cities! In the city of New Jerusalem, there will be nothing that is unholy.

THE SIZE OF THE CITY

You need to get some idea of the nature and dimension of the city to really appreciate it. It is beyond anything you've ever imagined. It is so great that only God could be the architect of this "city which has foundations, whose builder and maker is God" (Hebrews 11:10).

The size of New Jerusalem is amazing. Has anyone ever asked you, "How is Heaven going to be big enough so that all the Christians from all time will be able to live there?" It's going to be a massive place and unlike any other place you've ever known. To help us get an idea about it, an angel measured the city while on a walking tour with the apostle John.

And he who talked with me had a gold reed to measure the city, its gates, and its wall. The city is laid out as a square; its length is as great as its breadth. And he measured the city with the reed: twelve thousand furlongs. Its length, breadth, and height are equal.

—REVELATION 21:15, 16

39

The phenomenal size of this city—about fifteen hundred miles wide, fifteen hundred miles long, and fifteen hundred miles high—is one of the reasons that many people try to spiritualize it and just dismiss it as a symbol or a hypothetical place. The truth is, New Jerusalem is a city far beyond what we can imagine.

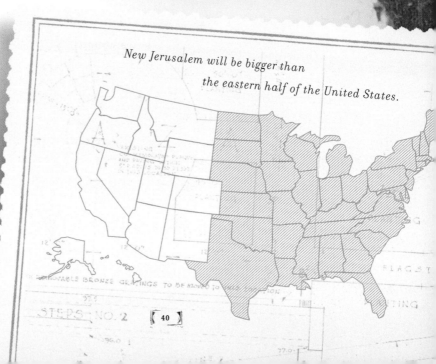

New Jerusalem will be bigger than the eastern half of the United States.

THE PEARLY GATES

Not only is it a holy city, but the Bible says it's an actual, physical place where the gates are made out of pearl. We didn't just make this up. This is not a myth. This is right from the Bible.

> [The city] had a great and high wall with twelve gates, and twelve angels at the gates, and names written on them, which are the names of the twelve tribes of the children of Israel . . . Then he measured its wall: one hundred and forty-four cubits, according to the measure of a man, that is, of an angel. The construction of its wall was of jasper; and the city was pure gold, like clear glass . . . The twelve gates were twelve pearls: each individual gate was of one pearl.
>
> —REVELATION 21.12, 17, 18, 21

You might be thinking, "That's some kind of an oyster to make pearls like that!" But, is God limited to building pearls only by oysters? I don't think so! If you want to find out more about how He did it, take Heaven's Pearly Gates Tour for a behind-the-scenes look at the creation of this wonder.

As you examine the twelve gates of pearl, you will see the names of the twelve tribes of Israel inscribed (Revelation 21:12). And the twelve gates are part of a wall that surrounds the city, glittering like a diamond bracelet.

> *The construction of its wall was of jasper; and the city was pure gold, like clear glass.*
>
> —REVELATION 21:18

When you see the New Jerusalem from afar, it will sparkle and shine, and the glory of the city will be so overwhelming, so breathtaking that you'll need heavenly sunglasses as you get close.

THE FOUNDATION
OF PRECIOUS STONES

After you see the pearly gates, you will notice that the foundations of the holy
city are of precious stones.

> *The foundations of the wall of the city were adorned with all kinds of*
> *precious stones: the first foundation was jasper, the second sapphire,*
> *the third chalcedony, the fourth emerald, the fifth sardonyx, the sixth*
> *sardius, the seventh chrysolite, the eighth beryl, the ninth topaz, the*
> *tenth chrysoprase, the eleventh jacinth, and the twelfth amethyst.*
> —REVELATION 21:19, 20

Those stones are all of the hues of the rainbow.

This great city will be built upon a twelve-layer foundation, and each of the
layers will be a different beautiful stone. When you see the foundation of the
city, you will be overwhelmed with the beauty of all of the gemstone
foundations underneath this gigantic city of God. Can you imagine?

A building's greatest strength is its foundation, and the New Jerusalem is not one foundation but twelve. Rather than being twelve individual foundations separated from each other, they are packed upon each other, and you see them all together in little ripples of gold and precious stones.

STREETS OF GOLD

The New Jerusalem is not only a holy city with pearly gates and foundation of precious stones but it's also a place where there are streets of gold. I know that some people think that's just folklore. You hear all about the streets of gold in heaven; we're going to walk on streets of gold. That description is in the old church spirituals, it's in the old gospel songs: the streets of gold. Are there really streets of gold in Heaven? Yes! That's what the Word of God says.

The construction of its wall was of jasper; and the city was pure gold, like clear glass . . . The twelve gates were twelve pearls, each individual gate was of one pearl. And the street of the city was pure gold, like transparent glass.

  —REVELATION 21:18, 21

Now, if you've ever looked at pure gold, you know that pure gold is not transparent, it's opaque. You can't see through pure gold. But John describes Heaven's city as transparent glass. The gold of Heaven is so pure that people seem to look through its clear depths as they walk upon it. It is finely polished as a mirror and therefore it is not so much transparent, but it is translucent.

As we think about this and wonder how a city could have pure-gold streets that we can see through, don't forget that in the glorified bodies that we will have then, our perceptions will be different. Something might appear to us then as being both solid and transparent. If we have glorified bodies, surely our eyesight will be different and completely enhanced, and we'll be able to see things as we've never seen them before. New Jerusalem will be a city with streets of gold that we can literally see through like we would look through a window pane. That's the best way to describe what John tells us. For more information about our abilities in our new bodies, see page 68.

THE LAMB THAT IS THE LIGHT

Beyond the glory of the city itself, we have the Lamb that is the Light.

> *. . . [The city's] light was like a most precious stone, like a jasper stone,*
> *clear as crystal . . . The city had no need of the sun or of the moon to*
> *shine in it, for the glory of God illuminated it. The Lamb is its light*
> —REVELATION 21:11, 23

In the New Jerusalem there will be no light sockets, there will be no lanterns, there will be no lamps. There will be the presence of light throughout the city that emanates from the Throne of God where sits the Lamb who is the Lord Jesus. The Bible says that in that city, He will be the light, and there will be no need for any other light because the brilliance of the Lord Jesus in His glorification will fill the city. Imagine that.

- No more electric bills!
- No glare from streetlights or headlights!
- No more pollution from power plants!

- No need to buy light bulbs!
- No sunscreen needed because the Son's light will not burn us.
- No carpets or clothes will become faded.
- Every living thing will receive the perfect amount of light.

This fulfills the prophecy of Isaiah recorded in chapter 60, verse 19:

The sun shall no longer be your light by day,
Nor for brightness shall the moon give light to you;
But the LORD will be to you an everlasting light,
And your God (will be) your glory.

This city doesn't reflect light due to any material combustion or consumption of fuel. It is from the Lamb, Himself, who is the Light of the World, and He will be the light of the city. No wonder Paul described our future like this as he said, "But as it is written: 'Eye has not seen, nor ear heard, nor have entered into the heart of man the things which God has prepared for those who love Him'" (1 Corinthians 2:9).

THE RIVER OF LIFE & THE TREE OF LIFE

Heaven has natural beauty, too, including a river and trees that you won't find anywhere else.

> *And he showed me a pure river of water of life, clear as crystal, proceeding from the throne of God and of the Lamb. In the middle of its street, and on either side of the river, was the tree of life, which bore twelve fruits, each tree yielding its fruit every month. The leaves of the tree were for the healing of the nations.*
>
> —REVELATION 22:1, 2

If you want to find the throne of God, all you'll have to do is follow the river, because the river flows from the throne. This river has been anticipated for a long time. Even the psalmist spoke of this river that is spoken about in the book of Revelation:

There is a river whose streams shall make glad the city of God.

—PSALM 46:4

On each side of this river are planted not just the tree, but the trees, of life. In the original Greek text, the word "tree" is a word used to mean a plurality of trees. In fact, there are twelve trees, and these trees bear different kinds of fruit each month throughout the year. We will be able to eat from every tree without prohibition.

Oh, what delight to try to imagine that beautiful city shining as a golden jewel with the water coming down from the throne of God and the trees of life planted on each side!

THE END OF THE OCEAN

In Heaven there will not be an ocean.

Now I saw a new heaven and a new earth, for the first heaven
and the first earth had passed away. Also there was no more sea.
—Revelation 21:1

You might say, "Well, I can't imagine a world that's beautiful without the sea."

But don't forget that in the New Jerusalem, there is a great river flowing down from the throne of God and running out into tributaries. This river is fresh water, not salt water. Salt is a preservative, and because there's no decay in the New Heavens and the New Earth, there'll be no need for salt. Instead, the fresh waters will flow throughout the world, and it will be more beautiful than anything you can imagine.

THE CITY SQUARE

Some cities have a town square, but the New Jerusalem is a square or rather, a cube. It is a city foursquare—about fifteen hundred miles wide, long, and high. The capital city of Heaven will have the potential to house all the people who have ever trusted in Christ from the very beginning of time, including all of those who have died before the age of accountability: all of the children who have died without having an opportunity to receive Christ and all of those who are not mentally capable of understanding the Gospel. This city will be large enough to house everyone.

It is big enough for everyone who will be there, but it won't be crowded. And not only that, but it will be a magnificently beautiful city like nothing we've ever seen. It will sparkle in the atmosphere. It will glow. It will draw us into itself. There is no earthly vocabulary great enough to help us understand it completely.

GOOD FOOD AND FELLOWSHIP

You and your friends, old and new, will find many venues for fellowship.
Dining together will be one of them. Heaven's Restaurant Row is certainly
splendid beyond comparison. There everyone enjoys a wonderful view and
the best companionship no matter where they sit.

It is a place characterized by laughter without
tears, life without death, singing without
mourning, contentment without crying, and
pleasure without pain. And our Lord and Savior,
Jesus Christ, will be there. And our loving
heavenly Father will be there. And the blessed
Holy Spirit will be there. It's the place to be!

It won't be difficult to find good food or
restful surroundings in which to enjoy fellowship. We will get
food much like Adam and Eve did in the Garden before the fall of mankind.
Currently, we have to labor and toil as we care for the ground, sow and reap
crops, and prepare food; but in Heaven, the ground will no longer produce

thorns and thistles. Instead there will be nothing but delicious nourishment without pesticides or growth hormones or bioengineering. All food will be healthy, and the flavor will be beyond what our taste buds can process outside of Heaven. You think that steak was good? Just wait!

We can eat all we want from any tree in Paradise, and we'll never gain weight or get tired of the flavors. We will eat for enjoyment and for the pleasure of it without bearing any of the human penalties that we now bear.

Because of man's fall into sin, a curse was pronounced over the earth. But God sent His Son into the world to redeem His creation from the results of sin, and the work of Christ is not just to save the innumerable throng of blood-bought people. The total work of Christ is nothing less than to redeem this entire creation from the effects of sin. That purpose will be accomplished in Heaven.

Paradise lost becomes paradise regained.

GOD'S THRONE ROOM

The center of worship in Paradise is the Throne Room of God. The word "throne" appears forty-six times in the book of Revelation, fourteen times in chapter 4. In this context, "throne" speaks of sovereignty, it speaks of authority, it speaks of reign, it speaks of control. And when we read in Revelation about the throne of God, it is a reminder that while the events of this earth seem to be chaotic and without any meaning, there is One in the universe who is seated on the throne.

We are not left directionless in this life. It may appear that no one is in control here; maybe you feel that way in your life. But Almighty God is seated on that throne in Heaven. He is sovereign, and He is in control, hallelujah!

After these things I looked, and behold, a door standing open in heaven . . . Immediately I was in the Spirit; and behold, a throne set in heaven, and One sat on the throne. And He who sat there was like a jasper and a sardius stone in appearance; and there was a rainbow around the throne, in appearance like an emerald.

—REVELATION 4:1-3

A door opened in Heaven, and John was able to look inside. He was able to see what no one has ever seen before. From his lonely exile on the Isle of Patmos, John saw the worship taking place around the throne in Heaven.

As John saw the throne in Heaven, he tried to describe it. He had a very difficult task, because the primary focus of the throne is God Himself, and the Bible says, "'No man shall see Me, and live'" (Exodus 33:20). John could only see the image of God, and he symbolically described what he saw as he looked through the door into Heaven. As he looked upon the throne, all he could see was the brilliance of a diamond (jasper), a ruby (sardius stone), an emerald, and a rainbow all rolled into one. It was so magnificent, it took his breath away.

Like John, the door to Heaven will open for us, and we will be as hard pressed as John was to describe the glory within. But it will be something like what he has described. The brilliance and beauty and glory of that place will amaze us and remind us that God is not on vacation. He hasn't taken a sabbatical. God is on the throne. He is seated in His majesty there, in Heaven.

THE WORSHIP IN GOD'S THRONE ROOM

John was allowed to see heavenly worship, and he gives us a glimpse of what it will be like, someday, to be a part of that great worship experience when, forever, we will bring honor and glory to our God.

> *Around the throne were twenty-four thrones, and on the thrones I saw twenty-four elders sitting, clothed in white robes; and they had crowns of gold on their heads . . . Whenever the living creatures give glory and honor and thanks to Him who sits on the throne, who lives forever and ever, the twenty-four elders fall down before Him who sits on the throne and worship Him who lives forever and ever, and cast their crowns before the throne.*
>
> —REVELATION 4:4, 9, 10

John tried to describe what he saw and heard. He witnessed massive, overwhelming, magnificent, glorious praise of the God in Heaven. He recorded the text of the song of the twenty-four elders who represent the church of the Living God.

"You are worthy to take the scroll,

And to open its seals;

For You were slain,

And have redeemed us to God by Your blood

Out of every tribe and tongue, and people and nation,

And have made us kings and priests to our God;

And we shall reign on the earth."

—REVELATION 5:9, 10

One day we will be part of the gathering around that throne in the very center of Heaven, and we will give Him glory.

Knowing that we're going to spend eternity in praise and worship around the throne should challenge us, His people, to take seriously the biblical instruction on worship and continue to grow in our ability to worship and praise God. What we are learning to do in our short time on this earth, we will spend an eternity doing in Heaven.

THREE HEAVENS

Did you know there are three Heavens? You say, "Man, I'm trying to figure out one; you tell me there's three?" Yes. There are three heavens in the Bible.

> *I know a man in Christ who fourteen years ago—whether in the body I*
> *do not know, or whether out of the body I do not know, God knows—*
> *such a one was* CAUGHT UP TO THE THIRD HEAVEN.
>
> 2 CORINTHIANS 12:2 EMPHASIS ADDED

The first Heaven is what we might call the atmospheric Heaven, that blanket of air immediately surrounding our earth in which birds and clouds move, and it's mentioned in Scripture a number of times.

> *For as the heavens are higher than the earth,*
> *So are My ways higher than your ways,*
> *And My thoughts than your thoughts.*
>
> —ISAIAH 55:9

Then God said, "Let the waters abound with an abundance of living creatures, and let birds fly above the earth across the face of the firmament of the heavens."

—Genesis 1:20

The second Heaven refers to the stellar heaven that contains the sun, the moon, the stars and all of the galaxies other than our own.

Then God said, "Let there be lights in the firmament of the heavens to divide the day from the night; and let them be for signs and seasons, and for days and years; and let them be for lights in the firmament of the heavens to give light on the earth"; and it was so. Then God made two great lights: the greater light to rule the day, and the

lesser light to rule the night. He made the stars also. God set them in

the firmament of the heavens to give light on the earth.

—Genesis 1:14-17

But Paul tells us there is something beyond the atmospheric Heaven and the stellar Heavens; there is a third Heaven, and it is the place that God resides.

The Lord is in His holy temple,

The Lord's throne is in heaven.

—Psalm 11:4

It is to that Heaven of heavens that we aspire. It is that third Heaven where we are going some day to be with God and to be with Jesus Christ.

This is Paradise.

WHAT ABOUT THE CHILDREN?

Many people worry about what happens to little children who die before they can understand the Gospel, but in the Bible we have several assurances that they go straight to Heaven. These principles also apply to people whose bodies may be mature, but whose minds have been impaired to such an extent that they have the mind of a child.

1. THE CHARACTER OF GOD—That God is given the name, "Father," ought to tell us something. We also know He is "full of compassion, and gracious, longsuffering and abundant in mercy and truth" (Psalm 86:15).

When the Israelites wouldn't believe that God could help them go into the Promised Land, the adults of that generation were not allowed to go there, but the children were exempted from that penalty (Deuteronomy 1:39).

God says all children are His children (Ezekiel 16:20), and He refers to these little ones as innocents (Jeremiah 2:34, Jeremiah 19:4). Although children are sinful creatures, just like all of us, they are not responsible in the same way as people whose sins are willful and premeditated. In that sense God refers to them as innocents.

2. THE CONDITION FOR SALVATION—All of the threats of

hell in the Bible are reserved for people who have sinned knowingly and willingly. Galatians 5:19-21 speaks of those who end up in hell, and it gives a long list of all the things that they do to deny the holiness of God Revelation 21:8 has a similar list, but much shorter. These verses speak of lifestyle choices to continue to reject God's grace.

In one of his prophecies about the Lord, Isaiah refers to a period of moral innocence in the life of a child. "For before the Child shall know to refuse the evil and choose the good, the land that you dread will be forsaken by both her kings" (Isaiah 7:16). There's a period of time when children don't understand the difference between good and evil and when they cannot yet comprehend the Gospel. During that period of time, these children are protected under the blood of the Lord. If a child is not capable of rejecting the Gospel, then certainly, God has provided for him in grace.

3. THE COMPASSION OF THE SAVIOR—When you study the life of the Lord Jesus, you discover at once that He had an incredible love for little children, and He demonstrated that love on so many different occasions (Matthew 19:13, 14; Mark 10:13, 14; Luke 18:15-17; Matthew 18:5, 14). The Lord Jesus has compassion for little children and infants and is not willing that even one of them should perish. This includes babies that are never born because of miscarriages or abortions.

4. THE CHILD OF DAVID—King David's adultery with Bathsheba resulted in a child. As punishment for their sin, the prophet Nathan foretold that the boy would die. While the baby was sick, David fasted and wept; but after the child died, "David arose from the ground, washed and anointed

himself, and changed his clothes; and he went into the house of the LORD and worshiped" (2 Samuel 12:20). David's behavior stunned his servants, but he explained that he was cheered by the fact that one day he would be reunited with the baby in Heaven. "Now he is dead; why should I fast? Can I bring him back again? I shall go to him, but he shall not return to me" (verse 23).

David knew something that we now know: When little children die before they understand the Gospel, they go straight to Heaven. The tenor of the Word of God, the character of God, and the consequences of believing all bring together this truth that children who die before they can understand the Gospel, go to Heaven.

So at what age do children become responsible for their relationship with God? Whenever they are able to understand God's love. When they comprehend what it means to be a sinner. For some children, that knowledge comes at a very early age, and for others it takes more time. The age of spiritual accountability is not a chronological measurement; it is a reckoning of spiritual understanding.

COMMUNITY OF HEAVEN:
What We'll Be

BECOMING A CITIZEN

Heaven won't be just our new residence; it will be our new nationality. "For our citizenship is in Heaven, from which we also eagerly wait for the Savior, the Lord Jesus Christ" (Philippians 3:20). Our native citizen status will be changed. We will receive our new passports and will be able to say, "I truly belong in Heaven." That's why Paul tells us, "Set your affection on things above, not on things on the earth" (Colossians 3:2 KJV). We're going home and we'll be there with Jesus, forever.

Our Redeemer is in Heaven, our relationships are in Heaven, our resources are in Heaven, our residence is in Heaven, our reward is in Heaven.

"Rejoice and be exceedingly glad, for great is your reward in heaven."
—MATTHEW 5:12

THE ULTIMATE MAKEOVER!
BEHOLD YOUR HEAVENLY BODY!

Among the benefits of being a citizen of Heaven is the complete makeover that everyone receives. All the people in Paradise are healthy, strong, vibrant. We call this makeover program Bodies by Jesus because the Lord is going to give us bodies better than we can imagine!

In 1 Corinthians, chapter 15, Paul gives us some contrasts between our current bodies and the bodies that we'll have in Heaven. Here are just some aspects of this ultimate extreme makeover:

- You will literally be in a brand-new resurrection body.
- You will completely leave behind every wrinkle.
- You will completely leave behind every illness.
- You will completely leave behind every bit of your body that isn't perfect.
- You will physically become like Jesus.

We're all pretty well acquainted with the kind of bodies that we now occupy and how many hours we have to take every week just to keep these bodies going. And as we age, our bodies need even more work. At the gym, many of us are constantly reminded that we have to work twice as hard to maintain the same level of fitness as we used to have earlier in life. Does that depress you a bit?

When your life is so busy and you need more and more time, you've got to take more and more of that time just to stay even, just so you don't fall behind! Our physical condition matters to all of us to some degree, as well it should. This is the case especially because our bodies are the temples that God has given us, and we're supposed to take care of them. But wouldn't you agree that taking care of your temple sometimes seems like a full-time job?

The apostle Paul gives us some encouragement in a broad outline in 1 Corinthians that tells us about our new bodies.

1. Our New Bodies Will Be Indestructible

Paul describes four different qualities of the resurrection body, and he contrasts it with this present body. So our new bodies will be indestructible. "So also is the resurrection of the dead. The body is sown"—and when you see the word "sown" here it means "buried"—"The body is [buried] in corruption, it is raised in incorruption" (1 Corinthians 15:42).

Our new bodies are not like our old bodies. Our current bodies wear out. We get old; we begin to notice that our parts don't work as they once did. We discover that no matter what we try and no matter what the infomercials promise, we can't stop the aging process.

You can listen to people pitch all of these products, call their toll-free numbers, and buy everything they offer. And you know what? It won't work! Because you cannot stop the body from aging. You can slow it down or camouflage it, but you can't stop it!

Our present bodies are buried in corruption, but our resurrection bodies are incorruptible. They are not capable of deterioration or decay. When we get our new bodies, they're bodies for life! They're bodies for eternity! These new bodies will never get old. They will never get tired. What shall be then shall be forever! We will be what we will be forever and ever. Our resurrection bodies will not be subject to accident or disease or age. We will be free from pain and decay and death. Our bodies will never wear out and will never die. Our new bodies will outlive the stars.

Are you ready for a body like that? Wow!

If your knees won't take the pounding you used to give them while running or your back can't take it when you ride a bike, you won't have to worry about those aches and pains EVER AGAIN! When you get to Heaven, you will be able to run with ease because you will have a perfect, indestructible, non-wear-out-able body. Your extreme makeover makes you indestructible!

2. Our New Bodies Will Be Identifiable

Our new bodies will be identifiable. Just as Mary Magdalene, Thomas, and the other disciples recognized Jesus, our friends and family will know us, and we will know them (John 20:11-29).

Identifiable, but glorious. You're still YOU, but so much better!

Our present bodies will be "sown" or buried, "in dishonor." But our new bodies will be "raised in glory" (1 Corinthians 15:43). The word "glory" really means "brilliance," and our new bodies will be glorious like the glorious body of the risen Savior. Notice the key phrase about what our bodies are going to be like:

> *For our citizenship is in heaven, from which we also eagerly wait for the Savior, the Lord Jesus Christ, who will transform our lowly body that it may be* CONFORMED TO HIS GLORIOUS BODY, *according to the working by which He is able even to subdue all things to Himself.*
> —PHILIPPIANS 3:20, 21 EMPHASIS ADDED

The glory that the Lord Jesus had in His glorious body is the glory we're going to have in our bodies when we are resurrected to Heaven.

BODY BY JESUS

When we're told that we are raised in glory, we can be confident in what that means. Our new bodies will be just like the resurrected body of the Lord Jesus Christ.

> *Beloved, now we are children of God; and it has not yet been revealed what we shall be, but we know that when He is revealed, we shall be like Him, for we shall see Him as He is.*
>
> —1 JOHN 3:2

Paul reiterates this powerful thought at the end of his teaching in 1 Corinthians, chapter 15: "As we have borne the image of the man of dust"—that's our current body—"we shall also bear the image of the heavenly Man" (verse 49).

That's Jesus. Just as our bodies now bear the images of Adam, one day we're going to bear the image of Jesus! We're going to have a body like His. That's why our makeover program is called "Body by Jesus." No workout program will ever top this one!

MORE ABOUT 'BODY BY JESUS'

We can observe what the "Body by Jesus" is like by reading about the times He appeared during the forty days between His resurrection and His return to Heaven. We can study those passages in the Bible to learn some things about Jesus' body, and by extension we'll also know what our resurrection bodies will be like.

1. THE RESURRECTION BODY IS REAL.

Jesus had a real body after His resurrection. This is important. Jesus said He had a real body.

> *Behold My hands and My feet, that it is I Myself. Handle Me and see, for a spirit does not have flesh and bones as you see I have.*
> —LUKE 24:39

Then He said to Thomas, "Reach your finger here, and look at My hands; and reach your hand here, and put it into My side. Do not be unbelieving, but believing."

—JOHN 20:27

Some alternate spiritual communities may claim to give you a new body, but read the fine print—they will try to convince you that you will only need a "virtual body." But in Paradise everything is one hundred percent real; you're not going to have some spirit-body that floats around forever. Jesus promised you're going to have a real body! He assured his friends, "Handle me. My body is real." And a spirit-body is an oxymoron. There isn't such a thing. Either you have a body, or you don't. If you exist only in the spirit, you're not in the body. Jesus' body was real, and when we get to Heaven we're going to have real bodies—real, transformed bodies like the body of the Lord Jesus when He was resurrected from the grave.

"Body by Jesus" means having a real body.

2. YOUR RESURRECTION BODY WILL ENJOY FOOD WITHOUT ANY NEGATIVE SIDE EFFECTS.

Our bodies, after their extreme makeovers, are going to be like our current bodies, only totally renovated, resurrected, made over. And because these bodies will be real, we'll be able to eat. This assurance will greatly encourage many of us. One of the most frequently asked questions is, "Are we going to eat in Heaven?"

Jesus, in His resurrected body, ate with His friends on at least two occasions after His resurrection. Once was when He first appeared to the disciples after His resurrection, and another time Jesus made breakfast and ate it with His disciples.

> *So they gave [Jesus] a piece of a broiled fish and some honeycomb. And He took it and ate in their presence.*
> —LUKE 24:42, 43

> *Jesus said to them, "Come and eat breakfast." Yet none of the disciples dared ask Him, "Who are You?"—knowing that it was the Lord. Jesus then came and took the bread and gave it to them, and likewise the fish.*
> —JOHN 21:12, 13

Eating is not just to keep your body alive, but it's a pleasurable experience. In Heaven we will be able to eat without any of the negative affects. No acid-reflux. No guilty fat grams. And chocolate will have no greater effect on our waistlines than fruit will. We'll be able to enjoy eating as if we'd never done it before.

But another great feature of Heaven is that although you'll be able to eat, you won't have to eat. You will eat for pleasure, not for survival. You'll be sustained by the power of God that resides within you. In the Garden of Eden, we had a picture of the beauty of uninterrupted cuisine, and in Heaven that scenario will be created again for us.

3. YOU WILL LOOK LIKE YOURSELF—ONLY BETTER!

Something people often ask is: "In my new body, will people know me? And will I know others?" The answer is "Yes!" Jesus, in His resurrection body, was real. His friends knew who He was.

Mary Magdalene was the first person who saw Jesus after His resurrection, and her grief turned to joy. We can imagine that she immediately leaped to hug Him, but then Jesus said to her, "Do not cling to Me, for I have not yet ascended to My Father; but go to My brethren and say to them, 'I am ascending to My Father and your Father, and to My God and your God'" (John 20:17).

The disciples knew that the Jesus who was with them after His death and resurrection was also the same Jesus they had known before his death. They knew this so deeply in their hearts and minds that they went to their deaths still proclaiming the reality of His resurrection. The same Jesus who died and was buried also was resurrected. They knew Him before the cross, and they knew Him after the Resurrection. He was the same person.

And that's the way it will be for us. When we get to Heaven, we're going to know all of the people whom we met on earth, and they're going to know us. The difference will be that all of our relationships in Heaven will be deeper and more loving than we can experience here.

> *For now we see in a mirror, dimly,*
> *but then face to face. Now I know in*
> *part, but then I shall know just as I*
> *also am known.*
>
> —1 CORINTHIANS 13:12

4. YOU WON'T BE LIMITED BY YOUR BODY.

The bodies we were born with are limited to the space they occupy, but our new bodies will be able to do things beyond the limits of both space and imagination. Like eternity, Heaven is really big. So, how are we going to get around in a place that huge? That's where our new bodies will be really helpful. We won't have to use normal transportation; all we'll have to say is, "I want to be in room seven on the six hundredth floor," and zap! We're there! Because we'll each have a glorified body that works like the body of the Lord Jesus, we will be able to travel the way He did.

On one occasion, Jesus entered a room without going through the door. He just appeared in the midst of His disciples.

The same day at evening, being the first day of the week, when the doors were shut where the disciples were assembled, for fear of the Jews, Jesus came and stood in the midst, and said to them, "Peace be with you."
  —JOHN 20:19

In our new bodies, we'll be able to arrive in a place without walking through the door. We will not have limitations like we have today. In Jesus' resurrection body He surmounted the limitations of this life. Earth had no power to stop Him, and our bodies are going to be the same.

Getting around is never going to be a problem again.

UNIVERSAL HEALTH PLAN

In the Bible, it says that the leaves of the tree of life are for healing of the nations (Revelation 22:2). The word "healing" in the Greek language is the word *therapeia*; it's the word from which we get "therapeutic." It means that we'll be able to eat the leaves of the tree, and the leaves will give us a greater sense of our lives and presence there. It will not enhance our holiness because we already will be perfectly holy, but it will give us a greater sense of enjoyment. It is therapeutic. Is this phenomenal or what!

GREAT IS YOUR REWARD

On earth we have Academy Awards, Choice Awards, Prism Awards, Screen Actors Guild Awards, Country Music Awards, Grammy Awards, Soap Opera Digest Awards, and on and on. But there's an award day coming with trophies to be given out like the world has never, ever dreamed of.

Talking about rewards in Heaven makes a lot of people nervous because there's this mentality that if we're living for God out of the love of our hearts, why would we want or need any awards? Somehow it doesn't seem spiritual to be looking for a reward. But God wants us to be faithful, and He helps motivate us to stay faithful by promising to give us crowns and rewards when we get to Heaven.

Some people say we should not be lured into goodness by promises of a bonus, for goodness is its own reward. While that argument sounds logical and moral, it is entirely out of harmony with what the Bible teaches. The Bible never defends the concept of rewards; rather, the idea is accepted as if it is the most natural and normal thing for us to expect.

BIBLE-BASED REWARDS

Rewards are assumed to be a part of the Christian's future experience. As you read through the Bible, starting even with the Old Testament, you discover that reward is a common theme. And as you read the Bible with that in mind, things start jumping off the page, everywhere you go.

In the Old Testament are Scriptures like these:

> *So that men will say,*
> *"Surely there is a reward for the righteous;*
> *Surely He is God who judges in the earth."*
> —PSALM 58:11

> *Also to You, O Lord, belongs mercy;*
> *For You render to each one according to his work.*
> —PSALM 62:12

Early in the New Testament is the Beatitudes with the Lord's promise of rewards. For instance:

"Blessed are you when they revile and persecute you, and say all kinds of evil against you falsely for My sake. Rejoice and be exceedingly glad, for great is your reward in Heaven."

—MATTHEW 5:11, 12

When you go all the way through the New Testament and you come to the last book in the Bible, Revelation 22:12 says, "'And behold, I am coming quickly, and My reward is with Me, to give to every one according to his work.'"

God is not unjust to forget your work and your labor of love which you have shown toward His name.

—HEBREWS 6:10-12

So [Jesus] said to them, "Assuredly I say to you, there is no one who has left house or parents or brothers or wife or children for the sake of the kingdom of God, who shall not receive many times more in this present time, and in the age to come eternal life."

—LUKE 18:29, 30

For whoever gives you a cup of water to drink in My name, because you belong to Christ, assuredly, I say to you, he will by no means lose his reward.

—MARK 9:41

So Jesus answered and said, "Assuredly, I say to you, there is no one who has left house or brothers or sisters or father or mother or wife or children or lands, for My sake and the gospel's, who shall not RECEIVE A HUNDREDFOLD *now in this time—houses and brothers and sisters and mothers and children and lands, with persecutions—and in the age to come, eternal life.*

—MARK 10:29, 30 EMPHASIS ADDED

Very few people on earth ever receive a hundredfold on any of our investments. But when we serve the Lord, He promises to reward us both in this life and in the life to come.

HEAVEN'S AWARDS

On the Judgment Day, one by one we are going to be judged by the Lord Jesus at the Judgment Seat, not for our salvation, but for what we have done as believers between the moment of our salvation and when we ultimately stand before Him. We will be rewarded not for the works that we've done in order to be saved, but for the works that we've done because we are saved!

> *For by grace you have been saved through faith, and that not of yourselves; it is the gift of God, not of works, lest anyone should boast. For we are His workmanship,* CREATED IN CHRIST JESUS FOR GOOD WORKS, *which God prepared beforehand that we should walk in them.*
> —EPHESIANS 2:8-10 EMPHASIS ADDED

When we stand before the Judgment Seat of Christ, it's not about whether we're going to get into Heaven or not. It will be about, "How have I lived my life as a believer?" "What kind of a steward have I been for the gifts that God has entrusted to me?"

As we anticipate our rewards in Heaven, though, it's important to keep these three concepts in mind:

1. Remember that the Lord Himself is your greatest reward.

After these things the word of the LORD came to Abram in a vision, saying, "Do not be afraid, Abram. I am your shield, your exceedingly great reward."

—GENESIS 15:1

Whatever else you may get in Heaven, the Lord himself is your chief reward—Heaven is where Jesus is. Whatever words you may use to describe Paradise is secondary to this fact: Heaven is where Jesus is. The Bible has many references to His presence there, and when we read it or hear it, the Bible leaves no question about the matter. When we go to Heaven, we are going to be with Jesus.

"And if I go and prepare a place for you, I will come again and receive you to Myself . . ." Why? ". . . [so] that where I am, there you may be also."

—JOHN 14:3

Heaven's not about the place; it's about the Person!

It's not about Heaven so much as it is about Jesus. It's about being with Him.

You'll get the best blessing in all eternity from this. You'll be so excited to know that the Jesus who walks with you every day, the One you talk with all the time in prayer, will be with you. And you will be with Him, permanently, in intimate personal fellowship.

2. *Resist doing works outwardly for the purpose of receiving a reward. If you serve the Lord just so you can get a reward, it indicates that you do not understand Christianity. Why do you serve the Lord? Because you love Him!*

> *When you do a charitable deed, do not let your left hand know what your right hand is doing, that your charitable deed may be in secret; and your Father who sees in secret will Himself reward you openly.*
>
> —MATTHEW 6:3, 4

3. *Reflect upon the ultimate goal of any rewards we may receive.*

> *The twenty-four elders fall down before Him who sits on the throne and worship Him who lives forever and ever, and cast their crowns before the throne.*
>
> —REVELATION 4:10

After we get all our rewards and we're going to be so excited about them, then we're going to see Jesus. And we're going to give Him back the only possessions we have in Heaven—the rewards and crowns He's given us. We're going to fall down at His feet and say, "Thank You, Lord, for enabling me to be here. Thank You, Lord, for paying for my sin. Thank You, Lord, for being my Redeemer. I haven't got much to give You, but here's my crown."

Another part of our heavenly reward will be to reign and rule with Christ upon this earth, and each of us will have opportunities to serve the Lord based upon our faithfulness in serving Him right now.

THE FIVE CROWN REWARDS CLUB

The Bible describes some of the prestigious awards awaiting us in Heaven, and among those awards are five crowns that are listed in the New Testament. These crowns are won by people who fulfill certain requirements while here on earth. When you make your RSVP for Heaven, you become eligible to participate in the prestigious Five Crown Rewards Club. There are five different features and awards for those who qualify:

- The Victor's Crown
- The Crown of Rejoicing
- The Crown of Life
- The Crown of Righteousness
- The Crown of Glory

These crowns from God are far more significant than mere accessories or jewelry. The Bible says we're going to cast those crowns at the feet of Jesus in an act of worship that will be unlike anything we have ever experienced before (Revelation 4:10). We won't want to be empty-handed that day; we'll want to have as many crowns as possible to offer in honor of our King.

THE VICTOR'S CROWN

Everyone who competes for the prize is temperate in all things. Now they
do it to obtain a perishable crown, but we for an imperishable crown.
Therefore I run thus: not with uncertainty. Thus I fight: not as one who
beats the air. But I discipline my body and bring it into subjection, lest,
when I have preached to others, I myself should become disqualified.

    –1 CORINTHIANS 9:25-27

Here's a little background to the experience that Paul writes about in
1 Corinthians. The Greeks had two major athletic festivals—the Olympic Games
and the Isthmian Games. The Isthmian Games were held at Corinth and would
therefore be very familiar to the Corinthian church who received Paul's letter.
Contestants in the games had to prove themselves in rigorous training for ten
months. The last month was spent in Corinth with supervised daily workouts in
the gymnasium and athletic fields. The race was always a major attraction at the
games, and that is the figure Paul uses to illustrate the faithful Christian life.

Those who run in a race all run, but one receives the prize.

    –1 CORINTHIANS 9:24

No one would train so hard for so long without intending to win. Yet out of the large number of runners in the Isthmian Games, only one could win the crown, which was made of leaves. "The prize" indicates that the apostle had in mind service and rewards, not salvation and life. Paul is observing that athletes who expect to win must train diligently.

Isthmian athletes disciplined themselves to win an insignificant prize that literally would wither away. Christians can win an incorruptible, unperishing prize, so shouldn't we be far more motivated than athletes? Paul's point, of course, relates to personal discipline. Walking with God demands personal sacrifice. We must be prepared to sacrifice things that are not necessarily evil, but which prevent our full devotion to God.

In an age of abundance, Paul's words have special significance for serious-minded servants of Jesus Christ. If you want to win an award, if you want to receive a crown, you're going to have to say "No" to some things so that you can say "Yes" to other things. You can't live the pleasure-gorged life that our culture says is normal today. You have to turn off the television sometimes so you can study the Word of God. You have get up in the morning earlier than you want to so you can get with God and be ready for the day. You have to take time away from other things you want to do so that you can memorize Scripture and store it in your heart. You've got to change your schedule sometimes to go talk to somebody about Jesus.

These are difficult things to do, but the Bible says that people who won't discipline themselves to make such sacrifices can't be candidates for the victor's crown. This award is given only to those who discipline their bodies, as Paul did, and who practice self-control. An athlete leads his body; he does not follow it. It is his slave, not the other way around. It is this kind of soldier who will win the victor's crown.

The Crown of Rejoicing

For what is our hope, or joy, or crown of rejoicing? Is it not even you in the presence of our Lord Jesus Christ at His coming?

—1 Thessalonians 2:19

Paul asked the Thessalonians this question: "What is our crown of rejoicing?" Then he answered it in the next phrase: "[It is] even you in the presence of our Lord Jesus Christ at His coming." What is Paul talking about? He was saying that the crown of rejoicing is the crown you get because you led someone to Christ. He was saying, "Thessalonians, let me tell you what the crown of rejoicing is; it's you! Because we ministered to you. And someday, when we stand before the Lord, you're going to be there because we had a ministry to you." Sometimes it's called the soul winner's crown. It's the crown that Almighty God gives to us when we stop thinking it's all about me! and we instead start looking around for people who need a touch from God. It's our reward for using the talents and gifts He's given us to reach out with the Gospel of Jesus Christ.

When was the last time you ever talked about Jesus to someone who wasn't a Christian? When was the last time you even thought about doing it?

Some people in the church are constant witnesses; they talk to people all the time about Jesus, and they're candidates for the crown of rejoicing. Paul's love for these believers is very emotional. He calls them his joy, his hope, and his crown. Their crown is the soul winner's crown.

THE CROWN OF LIFE

Blessed is the man who endures temptation; for when he has been
approved, he will receive the crown of life which the Lord has promised
to those who love Him.

—JAMES 1:12

Do not fear any of those things which you are about to suffer. Indeed,
the devil is about to throw some of you into prison, that you may be
tested, and you will have tribulation ten days. Be faithful until death,
and I will give you the crown of life.

—REVELATION 2:10

The crown of life is given in recognition of persevering and triumphing over trial
and temptation and persecution, even to the point of martyrdom. The motivation
for gaining this crown has to be love for Christ. So many people have endured
terrible struggles to preserve our faith, and in the early days of Heaven many of
those people will be walking around with crowns of life because of their
persecution for the cause of Christ.

I believe that in our culture today many Christians are entrusted with a great deal of suffering. Maybe you are one of them. But you endure it with the right spirit, you give glory to God, and you don't complain all the time. You don't always ask Him, "Why?" but you walk through the trials and carry yourself as a person of integrity and a true man or woman of God. Someday you'll stand before God and He will say, "You took it and you took it well, and you honored Me in the midst of it. Here's the crown of life."

Charles Wesley wrote a hymn about this:

> *In hope of that immortal crown,*
> *I now the cross sustain*
> *And gladly wander up and down,*
> *And smile at toil and pain:*
> *I suffer out my three-score years,*
> *Till my Deliverer come,*
> *And wipe away His servant's tears,*
> *And take His exile home.*

The Crown of Righteousness

I have fought the good fight, I have finished the race, I have kept the faith. Finally, there is laid up for me the crown of righteousness, which the Lord, the righteous Judge, will give to me on that Day, and not to me only but also to all who have loved His appearing.

—2 Timothy 4:7, 8

Paul was prepared to meet the Lord and certain of his own imminent death as he wrote the second letter to Timothy. He was content with his record of service and confident of his reception by the Savior. Paul describes his life in terms of an athletic victory. This metaphor is especially appropriate for the life of the believer because it describes struggle, endurance, discipline, and final victory. The crown of righteousness is reserved for those who long for the Lord Jesus, who look for Jesus to come back.

Paul wasn't like the people who say things like, "Why should I care about going to Heaven when I haven't even been to Hawaii yet?" Some people set their hearts on Heaven and set their hearts on seeing Jesus Christ. The people who will win the crown of righteousness are those who love the appearing of the Lord.

THE CROWN OF GLORY

When the Chief Shepherd appears, you will receive the crown of glory that does not fade away.

—1 PETER 5:4

The crown of glory is the "preachers' crown." This one is for those who are faithful shepherds of the people of God and for Christian leaders. God has reserved one out of the five crowns for those who are in leadership and who are shepherds of God's flock. And to earn this crown, you don't have to be a pastor or even on a church staff. For instance, maybe you lead a small group. You care about the people who come every week. You know who they are and what their challenges are, and you pray for them and shepherd them. You're in the running for the shepherd's crown, the crown of glory.

TREASURES IN THE BANK OF HEAVEN!

You have an inheritance in Heaven that is preserved for you. When God became your Father, He made you an heir. You have an inheritance, and Peter says that inheritance has gone ahead of you.

- It's preserved in Heaven, forever. It cannot ever go away.
- It's not going to be touched by inflation.
- It's not going to be hurt by any of the ups and downs that we experience economically on earth.
- It's got your name on it. It's your inheritance.
- Your most valuable resources are in Heaven.

Matthew 6:19-21 says that we're not to lay up treasures for ourselves on earth, where moth and rust destroy, where thieves break in and steal; but we should store our treasure in Heaven where nothing can destroy it and no one can steal it. Matthew also reminds us that where our treasure is, there our heart will be as well.

The only way you can get your treasure from here to Heaven is to invest in the things that are going there, and the only things that are going there from this earth are the souls of men and women and the Word of God. So, if you'd like to build a little equity in Heaven, invest yourself! No brokerage firm is necessary. Invest your personal resources, your talents and time

and treasures, in the eternal Word of God and the

eternal souls of people. Then when you get to Heaven, you're going to see all those treasures that went there before you.

If you've ever loved someone who has died—and if that person was a Christian—then you're already investing in the Bank of Heaven. Your relationships with other believers will last forever, and every time a loved one dies, you'll find yourself looking forward to Heaven more and more.

Blessed be the God and Father of our Lord Jesus Christ, who according to His abundant mercy has begotten us again to a living hope through the resurrection of Jesus Christ from the dead, to an inheritance incorruptible and undefiled and that does not fade away, reserved in heaven for you.
—1 PETER 1:3, 4

WHEN WILL WE GET THERE?

Whether or not you're a Christian, you're going to be alive somewhere forever and ever. Your soul does not sleep. The body sleeps, and the spirit goes to Paradise, now in the third Heaven.

> *And Jesus said to him, "Assuredly, I say to you,* TODAY *you will be with Me in Paradise."*
>
> —LUKE 23:43 EMPHASIS ADDED

When Jesus ascended after His death, He went into the earth and He took captivity captive (Ephesians 4:8-10). He went into the Paradise of the Old Testament, gathered all of the souls of believers who were there, and took them with Him up to the Third Heaven, the new Paradise. Paradise is no longer an intermediate place. However, Hades is the intermediate hell where the souls of unbelievers await the Great White Throne Judgement.

When believers die their souls go to be with Jesus. And on the day of resurrection, their bodies will come out of the grave and be transformed into permanent, heavenly bodies.

105

MAKING THE MOVE TO PARADISE: *What We'll Need*

TRAVEL ARRANGEMENTS AND ACCOMMODATIONS

To facilitate your journey to Paradise, a team of personal travel consultants will meet you where you are and guide you all the way there. The angels take you to Heaven! It's a beautiful picture to imagine. God sends His angels to take the believer to Paradise. For instance, Jesus told the story of what happened when a certain beggar died—one who had reservations in Heaven. He was carried all the way there by the angels (Luke 16:19-31).

It's not arrogant to say, "I know I'm going to Heaven." God gives us the gift of eternal life, and no one can ever take it away from us (John 10:29).

And He's offering you that gift today, whoever you may be. You don't want to miss Heaven, this wonderful place. The choice is up to you, and it's a decision you make in the here and now. As soon as you book your reservation, the elite customer service staff will break out in cheers! Immediately, plans will get under way in preparation for your arrival: Your name is entered into Heaven's registry book; your custom-built mansion begins construction; you become eligible to earn Heaven's rewards.

WE'LL BUY YOUR OLD HOME

Within the heart of every man and woman lies a longing for a golden age. This idea is expressed in the promises of politicians every year. You can hear it in the dreams of poets and read it in literature across the centuries. Many people have, from time to time, actually tried to produce utopian communities. This dream finds its expression in many beautiful passages in the Scripture, both in the Old Testament and in the New.

- Isaiah prophesies a time when there will be a new heaven and a new earth, and it will last forever (Isaiah 66:22).
- Isaiah also reports that this new heaven and this new earth will be so wonderful, so completely beautiful, that it will cause us to forget what we know about the Earth as it is today (Isaiah 65:17).
- Peter suggests that this new heaven and this new earth will be a place where righteousness dwells (2 Peter 3:13).
- The writer of Hebrews says that one day God is going to take this world, fold it up like a garment, then change everything (Hebrews 1:10-12).

But when we move to Paradise, this earth won't be just condemned and destroyed. God will restore our current home at the end of the millennium.

> *But the day of the Lord will come as a thief in the night, in which the heavens will pass away with a great noise, and the elements will melt with fervent heat; both the earth and the works that are in it will be burned up.*
> —2 PETER 3:10

The term "burned up" in this passage of Scripture does not appear that way in the early Greek manuscripts. The actual word in the text conveys the idea of being uncovered, or laid open for exposure. This means that Peter is talking about God purifying the earth, not destroying it. The basic materials of the earth's structure will not be annihilated but will undergo tremendous processes of disintegration. Then, using the basic material elements of the former earth, God will exercise His creative power and will create the new heavens and the new earth.

So in what sense will the new heavens and the new earth be new? Well, there are two words in the Greek language that are translated by the word "new." And the one that is translated here describes something that is new, not in time, but in quality. It describes something that has been renovated and refreshed from the ruin and defilement of the past.

He's going to destroy all the evidences of decay, disobedience, and disease still in the world—but He is not going to destroy the world. He's not going to annihilate the world in which you and I currently live; He's going to purify it.

Over and over again in Genesis chapter 1, as God completed every part of the creation, He "saw that it was good." And when he got all the way done, God saw that "indeed it was very good." There is no evidence that he has ever changed His mind. His purpose is not to abandon His creation; His purpose is to restore it.

Knowing that God will make this earth new changes our thinking in at least two ways:

1. *We have a new appreciation for the world in which we now live.* Christians have a reputation of being very poor ecologists. Too many of us believe that this world is going to be destroyed someday and that there's little reason to spend time trying to take care of it. But when we understand that this earth is not going to be destroyed, but refreshed, when we understand that this earth, somehow is going to be a part of our future we look at this world in a whole different way. God created a beautiful world. And yes, we've messed it up, but one day He's going to come back and fix it.

2. *We have a new appreciation of the world to which we're going.* Heaven is a place characterized by laughter without tears and life without death and singing without mourning and contentment without crying and pleasure without pain. Our Lord and Savior, Jesus Christ, will be there, and our loving heavenly Father will be there, and the blessed Holy Spirit will be there, and there will be a New Heaven and a New Earth crowned by a resplendent city called the New Jerusalem.

BEFORE YOU LEAVE
YOUR OLD HOME

The coming of Christ and the doctrine of Heaven provide some of the strongest motivation for living the Christian life that you will ever find; so as you prepare to move to your new home in Paradise, you'll find yourself living more and more in accordance with the principles of Heaven.

What you believe about the future determines how you live today. And the more you move yourself away from what God has planned for you in the future, the more apt you are to become a person who just sort of drifts through life. You see, when you know where you're going, it makes all the difference in the world how you live. If you keep reminding yourself that one day you're going to spend eternity with a holy God—and the only way you're going to get rewards in Paradise is through the service your render here—then living for Heaven makes all the difference in the world.

What we think about heaven determines how we live today. The future is like an anchor that has been cast ahead of us and it is pulling us into the future.

> *Therefore, beloved, looking forward to these things, be diligent to be found by Him in peace, without spot and blameless.*
> —2 PETER 3:14

We must be different people because of our exposure to God's Word. If we just float along with the culture, we will be victimized by it. We are not like everyone around us; we are not like the world in which we live. We're God's people! We're different! And because of our belief in Heaven, Hell, and the Second Coming, there are at least five things that Christians need to take seriously:

1. *Our purity is important.* When we read about the future, it always has an impact on the present. Because Jesus is coming back, we ought to be motivated to live in a more godly way (1 John 3:3).

2. *His promises are rock-solid truth.* Jesus is coming back. Philippians 3:20 says we're to eagerly wait for the Savior. Titus 2:13 says

we're to look for His coming. Hebrews 9:28 says we're to eagerly wait for His coming. Paul put it this way toward the end of his life: "Finally, there is laid up for me the crown of righteousness, which the Lord, the righteous Judge, will give to me on that Day, and not to me only but also to all who have..." what? "loved His appearing" (2 Timothy 4:8).

3. *Our purpose is clear.* In light of the fact that Jesus is coming back, be diligent about your purpose. Make sure you get up every day and think Christianly, "Gird up the loins of your mind" (1 Peter 1:13) around the thing God has called you to do and say, " This is what I'm all about." God has called you to do some things. And you know what? In order to say yes to some things, you've got to say no to some others.

4. *We must be steadfast to our profession of faith.* We cannot lose our salvation, but we can lose our strength in Him. "You therefore, beloved, since you know this beforehand, beware lest you also fall from your own steadfastness, being led away with the error of the wicked" (2 Peter 3:17). When we're steadfast, we know what we believe, we know why we believe it, and nothing can sway us from it. We're not just surface Christians, but the roots go down deep into our hearts.

5. *Our progress must continue.* In light of the fact that Jesus is coming back, we must "grow in the grace and knowledge of our Lord and Savior Jesus Christ" (2 Peter 3:18). For healthy physical growth, we've got to do things like eating right, exercising, and staying away from contaminants. Growing spiritually has a lot of the same principles, such as feeding on the Word, serving the Lord, and avoiding sin.

Confirming Your
Reservation in Heaven

DON'T MISS OUT ON THIS LIMITED-TIME OFFER!

Confirming your reservation to become a citizen of Paradise forever is easy. But it is a limited-time offer. You must RSVP while you are still on earth. This is the most important thing you'll ever do. It's clear who may enter Heaven's gated community: "only those who are written in the *Lamb's Book of Life*" (Revelation 21:27).

In Heaven there is a book, a registry. It's called the *Lamb's Book of Life*, and the names of all who will be in Heaven are recorded in that book. There's a place in that book for your name. Jesus encouraged His disciples, "'Nevertheless do not rejoice in this, that the spirits are subject to you, but rather rejoice because your names are written in heaven'" (Luke 10:20).

There's a way to make sure your name is written in Heaven. Do this, and you'll be able to say with authority to anyone on earth, "My name is in the book. I have made a reservation. I have put my trust in Jesus Christ as my Savior and, therefore, I qualify to come in."

In that same chapter of the Bible where Jesus said, "In My house are many mansions" (John 14:2), He also told us how to make a reservation to live in one of those mansions. That's the greatest of all good news: Almighty God is still accepting reservations for Heaven. If you've never put your trust in Christ, it's not too late.

> "But the cowardly, unbelieving, abominable, murderers, sexually immoral, sorcerers, idolaters, and all liars shall have their part in the lake which burns with fire and brimstone, which is the second death."
>
> —REVELATION 21:8

> But there shall by no means enter it anything that defiles, or causes an abomination or a lie, but only those who are written in the Lamb's Book of Life.
>
> —REVELATION 21:27

If you have committed any of these sins, you're not automatically excluded from Paradise. Rather, the Bible says that if sin is your lifestyle and you've never repented of it, thereby disregarding the forgiveness of God, you will never go to the holy city. The only people who get into the city are people whose names are written in the *Lamb's Book of Life*. No exceptions. If you have not accepted God's plan for your life and received His forgiveness for your sin, you will be denied entrance into Heaven. God loves you and wants to welcome you home, but He will not allow into that city anyone who refuses to acknowledge personal sin, affirm that Jesus paid the penalty for sin on the cross, and accept His forgiveness.

THE WAY TO HEAVEN

After Jesus told everybody He was going to Heaven, His disciple Thomas, who became known as the doubter, asked, "Lord, we do not know where You are going, and how can we know the way?" (John 14:5). In other words, where's the map? How exactly do we get there? Jesus spoke to all of the disciples as He reassured Thomas, saying, in essence, "I know you don't know where I'm going, and I know you don't know how to get there; but let me just put your heart at ease." Then He gave the most succinct of specific directions:

> *I am the way, the truth, and the life. No one comes to the Father except through Me.*
>
> —JOHN 14:6

Some people think it doesn't sound charitable to say that Jesus is the only way to Heaven. But if you miss Jesus, you miss getting a reservation in Heaven. Then one day you'll stand before the Guest Services Agent of Heaven and He'll tell you, "I can't find your name in the book. You'll have to leave." The Bible even gives us the script for that terrible moment. Jesus will say, "I never knew you; depart from Me" (Matthew 7:23).

The way you get to Heaven is by putting your trust in Jesus Christ. Whether you are traveling from the North, South, East, or West, there is just one route.

- Ask Him to forgive your sin and give you the gift of eternal life. God has promised that He will never turn away anyone who comes to the Lord believing through faith.
- You don't have to understand it all. Faith is not understanding everything. Faith is just believing the simple truth from God Almighty.
- God wants you to spend eternity with Him in Heaven, and all He wants you to do is believe that Jesus Christ came to this earth, died on the cross, and paid the penalty for all your sin. And because He was the God-man, He could die one-on-one for everybody who lives. His death was infinite. He was God dying on a cross for you and me. And He simply says, "Will you believe it? Will you accept it? Will you receive it?"
- If you will believe, you can be guaranteed in the here and now that you will spend eternity with God. You don't have to wait until you die to find that out. You can know it now.

THE SPECIAL OFFER

Today, Heaven's special offer is still open for you. Almighty God is inviting you to the banquet. He's inviting you to come and receive His forgiveness. He wants you to become a Christian by receiving Jesus Christ. On the cross, He died for you and paid the penalty for your sin. He was raised again the third day, and He offers salvation full and free to all who will put their trust in Him. Have you done that? Is your name written in the *Lamb's Book of Life*? If not, you can do it today. Just ask!

You are pre-approved for acceptance to become a member of the family of God. You can ask Him just by talking to Him in prayer in your own words, or pray one of the prayers in this book, like the short one below. It takes courage to do it, but if you call on Jesus today, you'll be taking the most important step in your life. To come to Christ, we must acknowledge that we need Him. This can be the moment when you just lift up your hand towards God and say . . .

"Lord, I need You. I need you. I want to be a Christian."

Amen!

RSVP PRAYER

Lord, help me not to gamble with eternity. Help me not to think that I can take care of this at a later time, when I have no guarantee that a later time will be granted. Help me, Lord, to know that if You've spoken in my heart today and I hear Your voice by the Holy Spirit, this is my defining moment. Come into my heart and cleanse me of all my sins. Create a new heart in me today as You will create a new home for me in Heaven. Live with me here on earth and help me follow You.

I ask this in Jesus' name.

Amen

*And the Spirit and the bride say,
"Come!" And let him who hears say,
"Come!" And let him who thirsts come.
Whoever desires, let him take the water
of life freely . . . He who testifies to
these things says, "Surely I am coming
quickly." Amen. Even so, come, Lord
Jesus! The grace of our Lord Jesus
Christ be with you all. Amen.*

—REVELATION 22:17, 20, 21

A NOTE ABOUT THIS BOOK

Sometimes we talk about Heaven flippantly in daily conversation. There are a lot of jokes about Heaven. But in all of the fun we have anticipating it, don't lose this truth: Heaven is a magnificent place created by God, the Creator of all. The Creator of creativity has saved His best work until the last, and He is creating for us a real place that is so phenomenal that we will be overwhelmed.

Some people caution, "Don't think about Heaven too much. You'll get so heavenly minded that you're no earthly good."

But that worry is false. People who really understand where they're heading

and how wonderful it is have a greater sense of purpose while they're on this

earth. When we come together as God's people, let's remind each other that

God has given us the privilege of being His real estate agents. Our purpose is

to go out into the hinterland and invite people to move to Paradise. Everyone

is welcome to participate in God's crown production, the heavenly Jerusalem,

by putting their trust and their faith in Jesus Christ.

HEAVENLY REAL ESTATE, INC.

David Jeremiah, *Agent*

ABOUT THE AUTHOR

Dr. David Jeremiah is Senior Pastor of Shadow Mountain Community Church in El Cajon, California. For ten years he served as President of San Diego Christian College in El Cajon. In 1998, he was appointed Chancellor. Dr. Jeremiah is also the host of the national radio program *Turning Point* which is broadcast daily on more than 950 stations. He received the Broadcaster of the Year Award for 2000 from National Religious Broadcasters; and since 1996, Dr. Jeremiah has served on the Board of Directors for that organization. In 2006, Turning Point received the Best Radio Teaching Program Award from the National Religious Broadcasters. Dr. Jeremiah holds a B.A. from Cedarville College, Cedarville, Ohio; a Th.M. from Dallas Theological Seminary; and a Doctorate of Divinity also from Cedarville.

Dr. Jeremiah has authored numerous books, including *When Your World Falls Apart, Escape the Coming Night, The Handwriting on the Wall* (co-written with C. C. Carlson), *Slaying the Giants in Your Life, Searching for Heaven on Earth,* and *The Secret of the Light* (with Thomas Kinkade). Dr. Jeremiah is also a frequent speaker for professional basketball, baseball, and football chapels. Dr. Jeremiah and his wife, Donna, have four children and eight grandchildren.

For more information about Dr. Jeremiah, his works, and his ministries, visit www.turningpointonline.org.